Demon Kings Magick

S ROB

DEDICATION

I dedicate this book to my mother and father.

CONTENTS

ACKNOWLEDGMENTS

I acknowledge the existence of real magick.

Chapter 1 Protection

In this book you will be learning how to summon all of the Kings of Hell simultaneously. It should be noted that all nine of the kings of Hell control many legions of demons and this means that through them we may gain a magical power we otherwise would not. But to summon them we will be using the assistance of the devil Leviathan. In fact, Leviathan is so large that he: really it: is often thought of as a large sea monster type creature and this is not that inaccurate when I add the point that the mouth of Leviathan is the gates of Hell itself: his mouth is the Hell Mouth. This means that when Leviathan opens his mouth, we can summon the Kings of Hell through and after we have talked to them, we may send them back again and get Leviathan to shut its mouth again. This means that although this magick is potent it isn't particularly difficult to perform. However first I think you need to understand the kings of Hell that you will be summoning.

1. Baal first King of Hell, commands 66 legions of demons

2. Paimon, King of Hell, commands 200 legions of demons

3. Beleth King of Hell, commands 85 legions of demons

4. Purson King of Hell, commands 22 legions of demons

5. Asmodai King of Hell, commands 72 legions of spirits

6. Vine King of Hell, commands 36 legions of demons

7. Balam King of Hell, commands 40 legions of demons

8. Zagan Great King and President of Hell, commands 33 legions of demons

9. Belial King of Hell, commands 80 legions of demons and 50 legions of spirits

You now have some understanding of this magick and so let us move on to performing our magick. But remember you must will this magick to work so that it shall because it is your strong human will that makes this possible. The first magick is for protection and here it is.

All Kings of Hell magick for protection

Leviathan powerful devil, great monster, you whose mouth is the very gateway to Hell itself. Leviathan I ask that you open your mouth the Hell Mouth that which is the gates of Hell. Leviathan open your mouth, Hell's Mouth, open the gates of Hell here and now: Leviathan opens it's mouth the gates of Hell are open wide open. I summon through the gates Baal first King of Hell, commander of 66 legions of demons, Paimon, King of Hell, commander of 200 legions of demons, Beleth King of Hell, commander of 85 legions of demons, Purson King of Hell, commander of 22 legions of demons, Asmodai King of Hell, commander of 72 legions of spirits, Vine King of Hell, commander of 36 legions of demons, Balam King of Hell, commander of 40 legions of demons, Zagan Great King and President of Hell, commander of 33 legions of demons and Belial King of Hell, he with 80 legions of demons and 50 legions of spirits at his

command. I ask that the first King of Hell Baal, King Paimon, King Beleth, King Purson, King Asmodai, King Vine, King Balam, Great King Zagan, and King Belial step through the gateway to this world: First King Baal, King Paimon, King Beleth, King Purson, King Asmodai, King Vine, King Balam, Great King Zagan, and King Belial do step through to this world. All Kings of Hell I ask that you protect me from all harm and all attacks no matter what the source and this is what I ask of you all. First King Baal, King Paimon, King Beleth, King Purson, King Asmodai, King Vine, King Balam, Great King Zagan, and King Belial agree to help and departs back through the gates. Leviathan powerful devil, great monster, you whose mouth is the very gateway to Hell itself. Leviathan I ask that you shut your mouth the Hell Mouth that which is the gates of Hell. Leviathan close your mouth, Hell's Mouth, shut the gates of Hell here and now: Leviathan closes it's mouth the gates of Hell are closed. So it is and will be.

4

I want you to know that with some small adaptations that this magick can be used to work on anyone you desire: and know well enough. In fact, it is easiest to work magick on someone if they are someone you know well enough to know what they look like and their name. Will what follows to work and it shall.

All Kings of Hell magick to protect a chosen person

Leviathan powerful devil, great monster, you whose mouth is the very gateway to Hell itself. Leviathan I ask that you open your mouth the Hell Mouth that which is the gates of Hell. Leviathan open your mouth, Hell's Mouth, open the gates of Hell here and now: Leviathan opens it's mouth the gates of Hell are open wide open. I summon through the gates Baal first King of Hell, commander of 66 legions of demons, Paimon, King of Hell, commander of 200 legions of demons, Beleth King of Hell, commander of 85 legions of demons, Purson King of Hell, commander of 22 legions of demons, Asmodai King of Hell, commander of 72 legions of spirits, Vine King of Hell, commander of 36 legions of demons, Balam King of Hell, commander of 40 legions of demons, Zagan Great King and President of Hell, commander of 33 legions of demons and Belial King of Hell, he with 80 legions of demons and 50 legions of spirits at his command. I ask that the first King of Hell Baal, King Paimon, King Beleth, King Purson, King Asmodai, King Vine, King Balam, Great King Zagan, and King Belial step through the gateway to this world: First King Baal, King Paimon, King Beleth, King Purson, King Asmodai, King Vine, King Balam, Great King Zagan, and King Belial do step through to this world. All Kings of Hell I ask that you protect state name of chosen person from all harm and all attacks no matter what the source and this is what I ask of you all. First King Baal, King Paimon, King Beleth, King Purson, King Asmodai, King Vine, King Balam, Great King Zagan, and King Belial agree to help and departs back through the gates. Leviathan

6

powerful devil, great monster, you whose mouth is the very gateway to Hell itself. Leviathan I ask that you shut your mouth the Hell Mouth that which is the gates of Hell. Leviathan close your mouth, Hell's Mouth, shut the gates of Hell here and now: Leviathan closes it's mouth the gates of Hell are closed. So it is and will be.

I think that most of us all wish to protect our family and we can do this through magick. Of course, partly the strongest protection we give our family is what we have taught them and how we have made them durable and a difficult target. But people have their own nature and we can help them through this magick.

All Kings of Hell magick to protect your family

Leviathan powerful devil, great monster, you whose mouth is the very gateway to Hell itself. Leviathan I ask that you open your mouth the Hell Mouth that which is the gates of Hell. Leviathan

open your mouth, Hell's Mouth, open the gates of Hell here and now: Leviathan opens it's mouth the gates of Hell are open wide open. I summon through the gates Baal first King of Hell, commander of 66 legions of demons, Paimon, King of Hell, commander of 200 legions of demons, Beleth King of Hell, commander of 85 legions of demons, Purson King of Hell, commander of 22 legions of demons, Asmodai King of Hell, commander of 72 legions of spirits, Vine King of Hell, commander of 36 legions of demons, Balam King of Hell, commander of 40 legions of demons, Zagan Great King and President of Hell, commander of 33 legions of demons and Belial King of Hell, he with 80 legions of demons and 50 legions of spirits at his command. I ask that the first King of Hell Baal, King Paimon, King Beleth, King Purson, King Asmodai, King Vine, King Balam, Great King Zagan, and King Belial step through the gateway to this world: First King Baal, King Paimon, King Beleth, King Purson,

King Asmodai, King Vine, King Balam, Great King Zagan, and King Belial do step through to this world. All Kings of Hell I ask that you protect my family from all harm and all attacks no matter what the source, protect them with your strongest powers and that of those you command and this is what I ask of you all. First King Baal, King Paimon, King Beleth, King Purson, King Asmodai, King Vine, King Balam, Great King Zagan, and King Belial agree to help and departs back through the gates. Leviathan powerful devil, great monster, you whose mouth is the very gateway to Hell itself. Leviathan I ask that you shut your mouth the Hell Mouth that which is the gates of Hell. Leviathan close your mouth, Hell's Mouth, shut the gates of Hell here and now: Leviathan closes it's mouth the gates of Hell are closed. So it is and will be.

You have now learnt some little and useful magick. The truth is that I feel we all should use the magick that you have just learnt because we all need protection before we do anything else. I am

proud of you.

Chapter 2 Cutting, burning and dismemberment

The magick in this chapter is violent this is because most curses are: although not always. The fact is we all need to be able to kick backside when needed. I therefore offer a helpful hint that if you cannot think of someone undeserving then by all means simply curse a dictator, they always deserve whatever curses they get. Here is magick to stab a chosen person.

All Kings of Hell magick to stab a chosen person

Leviathan powerful devil, great monster, you whose mouth is the very gateway to Hell itself. Leviathan I ask that you open your mouth the Hell Mouth that which is the gates of Hell. Leviathan open your mouth, Hell's Mouth, open the gates of Hell here and now: Leviathan opens it's mouth the gates of Hell are open wide open. I summon through the gates Baal first King of Hell, commander of 66 legions of demons, Paimon, King of Hell,

commander of 200 legions of demons, Beleth King of Hell,

commander of 85 legions of demons, Purson King of Hell,

commander of 22 legions of demons, Asmodai King of Hell,

commander of 72 legions of spirits, Vine King of Hell, commander

of 36 legions of demons, Balam King of Hell, commander of 40

legions of demons, Zagan Great King and President of Hell,

commander of 33 legions of demons and Belial King of Hell, he

with 80 legions of demons and 50 legions of spirits at his

command. I ask that the first King of Hell Baal, King Paimon, King

Beleth, King Purson, King Asmodai, King Vine, King Balam,

Great King Zagan, and King Belial step through the gateway to this

world: First King Baal, King Paimon, King Beleth, King Purson,

King Asmodai, King Vine, King Balam, Great King Zagan, and

King Belial do step through to this world. All Kings of Hell I ask

that you stab state name of chosen person again and again and this is what I ask of you all. First King Baal, King Paimon, King Beleth, King Purson, King Asmodai, King Vine, King Balam, Great King Zagan, and King Belial agree to help and departs back through the gates. Leviathan powerful devil, great monster, you whose mouth is the very gateway to Hell itself. Leviathan I ask that you shut your mouth the Hell Mouth that which is the gates of Hell. Leviathan close your mouth, Hell's Mouth, shut the gates of Hell here and now: Leviathan closes it's mouth the gates of Hell are closed. So it is and will be.

The following magick is to burn someone of your choosing I understand that being burnt is very painful and this is why if we have ever held a match too long that we drop it; imagine how painful it would be if it were all over and we could not drop it: this may well be the fate your chosen person has to put up with. Remember that cursing is real it is a real form of magical violence so don't perform this magick just as a joke: will it to work and it shall.

All Kings of Hell magick to burn a chosen person

Leviathan powerful devil, great monster, you whose mouth is the very gateway to Hell itself. Leviathan I ask that you open your mouth the Hell Mouth that which is the gates of Hell. Leviathan open your mouth, Hell's Mouth, open the gates of Hell here and now: Leviathan opens it's mouth the gates of Hell are open wide open. I summon through the gates Baal first King of Hell, commander of 66 legions of demons, Paimon, King of Hell, commander of 200 legions of demons, Beleth King of Hell, commander of 85 legions of demons, Purson King of Hell, commander of 22 legions of demons, Asmodai King of Hell, commander of 72 legions of spirits, Vine King of Hell, commander of 36 legions of demons, Balam King of Hell, commander of 40 legions of demons, Zagan Great King and President of Hell, commander of 33 legions of demons and Belial King of Hell, he with 80 legions of demons and 50 legions of spirits at his command. I ask that the first King of Hell Baal, King Paimon, King Beleth, King Purson, King Asmodai, King Vine, King Balam, Great King Zagan, and King Belial step through the gateway to this world: First King Baal, King Paimon, King Beleth, King Purson, King Asmodai, King Vine, King Balam, Great King Zagan, and King Belial do step through to this world. All Kings of Hell I ask that you burn <u>state name of chosen person</u> with the hottest flames and this is what I ask of you all. First King Baal, King Paimon, King Beleth, King Purson, King Asmodai, King Vine, King Balam, Great King Zagan, and King Belial agree to help and departs back through the gates. Leviathan powerful devil, great monster, you whose mouth is the very gateway to Hell itself. Leviathan I ask that you shut your mouth the Hell Mouth that which is the gates of Hell. Leviathan close your mouth, Hell's Mouth, shut the gates of Hell here and now: Leviathan closes it's mouth the gates of Hell are closed. So it is and will be.

This next curse is quite violent because it is for someone of your choosing to lose their arms and legs: for them to be cut off. The fact is however that they may not survive the loss of blood and may die. However, the large curses do not always work how you want them to and so just accept what effect you do get onto your chosen person.

All Kings of Hell magick to cut off the legs and arms of a chosen person

Leviathan powerful devil, great monster, you whose mouth is the very gateway to Hell itself. Leviathan I ask that you open your mouth the Hell Mouth that which is the gates of Hell. Leviathan open your mouth, Hell's Mouth, open the gates of Hell here and now: Leviathan opens it's mouth the gates of Hell are open wide open. I summon through the gates Baal first King of Hell, commander of 66 legions of demons, Paimon, King of Hell, commander of 200 legions of demons, Beleth King of Hell, commander of 85 legions of demons, Purson King of Hell, commander of 22 legions of demons, Asmodai King of Hell, commander of 72 legions of spirits, Vine King of Hell, commander of 36 legions of demons, Balam King of Hell, commander of 40 legions of demons, Zagan Great King and President of Hell, commander of 33 legions of demons and Belial King of Hell, he with 80 legions of demons and 50 legions of spirits at his command. I ask that the first King of Hell Baal, King Paimon, King Beleth, King Purson, King Asmodai, King Vine, King Balam, Great King Zagan, and King Belial step through the gateway to this world: First King Baal, King Paimon, King Beleth, King Purson, King Asmodai, King Vine, King Balam, Great King Zagan, and King Belial do step through to this world. All Kings of Hell I ask that you use all of your power to cut off the arms and legs of <u>state name of chosen person</u> and this is what I ask of you all. First King Baal, King Paimon, King Beleth, King Purson, King Asmodai, King Vine, King Balam, Great King Zagan, and King Belial agree to help and departs back through the gates. Leviathan powerful devil, great monster, you whose mouth is the very gateway to Hell itself. Leviathan I ask that you shut your mouth the Hell Mouth that which is the gates of Hell. Leviathan close your mouth, Hell's Mouth, shut the gates of Hell here and now: Leviathan closes it's mouth the gates of Hell are closed. So it is and will be.

You have now come to the end of this the second chapter. Of course, this means that you know more than the first chapter and yet still less than you will know after the others. What is here is an independent system of magick and yet it also can be used alongside and together with any form of occultism: magick: or indeed any sort of mundane non-magical effort you wish to use too. In fact, the best results in occultism are often gotten when we couple the

magical with the mundane. However never risk jail and so for now

you may be better utilizing this magick alone.

Chapter 3 Power and strength

I will now teach you about power and also strength. In fact, the truth of things is that life has been one long lesson about power and strength and why the owner of power and strength is almost always better off for possessing them. I will now show you how to work magick that will make you more powerful. However, I am not making a judgement on what sort of power you should get because all power is useful to us. The reason for this is that power can not just help us get what we want but usually one sort of power can readily be converted into another even if some little effort is required.

All Kings of Hell magick for greater power

Leviathan powerful devil, great monster, you whose mouth is the very gateway to Hell itself. Leviathan I ask that you open your mouth the Hell Mouth that which is the gates of Hell. Leviathan

open your mouth, Hell's Mouth, open the gates of Hell here and

now: Leviathan opens it's mouth the gates of Hell are open wide

open. I summon through the gates Baal first King of Hell,

commander of 66 legions of demons, Paimon, King of Hell,

commander of 200 legions of demons, Beleth King of Hell,

commander of 85 legions of demons, Purson King of Hell,

commander of 22 legions of demons, Asmodai King of Hell,

commander of 72 legions of spirits, Vine King of Hell, commander

of 36 legions of demons, Balam King of Hell, commander of 40

legions of demons, Zagan Great King and President of Hell,

commander of 33 legions of demons and Belial King of Hell, he

with 80 legions of demons and 50 legions of spirits at his

command. I ask that the first King of Hell Baal, King Paimon, King

Beleth, King Purson, King Asmodai, King Vine, King Balam,

Great King Zagan, and King Belial step through the gateway to this

world: First King Baal, King Paimon, King Beleth, King Purson,

King Asmodai, King Vine, King Balam, Great King Zagan, and King Belial do step through to this world. All Kings of Hell I ask that you help me to gain greater power and this is what I ask of you all. First King Baal, King Paimon, King Beleth, King Purson, King Asmodai, King Vine, King Balam, Great King Zagan, and King Belial agree to help and departs back through the gates. Leviathan powerful devil, great monster, you whose mouth is the very gateway to Hell itself. Leviathan I ask that you shut your mouth the Hell Mouth that which is the gates of Hell. Leviathan close your mouth, Hell's Mouth, shut the gates of Hell here and now: Leviathan closes it's mouth the gates of Hell are closed. So it is and will be.

This following magick exists solely to give you greater strength. However, this magick is at its best if you use it alongside other ways of becoming stronger. But I believe that most people should also think about movement because a strong but useless muscle is not beneficial and ideally, we would think of ourselves as athletes do and concentrate on the motions needed. Couple all of your methods together and you will find success comes easier.

All Kings of Hell magick for greater strength

Leviathan powerful devil, great monster, you whose mouth is the very gateway to Hell itself. Leviathan I ask that you open your mouth the Hell Mouth that which is the gates of Hell. Leviathan open your mouth, Hell's Mouth, open the gates of Hell here and now: Leviathan opens it's mouth the gates of Hell are open wide open. I summon through the gates Baal first King of Hell, commander of 66 legions of demons, Paimon, King of Hell, commander of 200 legions of demons, Beleth King of Hell, commander of 85 legions of demons, Purson King of Hell, commander of 22 legions of demons, Asmodai King of Hell, commander of 72 legions of spirits, Vine King of Hell, commander of 36 legions of demons, Balam King of Hell, commander of 40 legions of demons, Zagan Great King and President of Hell,

commander of 33 legions of demons and Belial King of Hell, he

with 80 legions of demons and 50 legions of spirits at his

command. I ask that the first King of Hell Baal, King Paimon, King

Beleth, King Purson, King Asmodai, King Vine, King Balam,

Great King Zagan, and King Belial step through the gateway to this

world: First King Baal, King Paimon, King Beleth, King Purson,

King Asmodai, King Vine, King Balam, Great King Zagan, and

King Belial do step through to this world. All Kings of Hell I ask

that you use your power to make me stronger and this is what I ask

of you all. First King Baal, King Paimon, King Beleth, King

Purson, King Asmodai, King Vine, King Balam, Great King Zagan,

and King Belial agree to help and departs back through the gates.

Leviathan powerful devil, great monster, you whose mouth is the

very gateway to Hell itself. Leviathan I ask that you shut your

mouth the Hell Mouth that which is the gates of Hell. Leviathan

24

close your mouth, Hell's Mouth, shut the gates of Hell here and now: Leviathan closes it's mouth the gates of Hell are closed. So it is and will be.

Robustness is a good thing to have because it makes us difficult to harm. You may wonder why I say this when the next magick is to make you impossible to hurt and the reason is that I do not expect it to give you its fullest power only a beneficial effect. Sometimes the best strategy is to shoot for the moon and accept whatever we get. But remember that as well as magick and being fit to make us more robust we also have vitamins and I myself have felt the beneficial effects of utilizing vitamin D3 alongside vitamin B12; at the moment I take both of these daily. However, there are other combinations that are beneficial and many experts put high regard to a multi-vitamin taken daily.

All Kings of Hell magick to be impossible to harm

Leviathan powerful devil, great monster, you whose mouth is the very gateway to Hell itself. Leviathan I ask that you open your mouth the Hell Mouth that which is the gates of Hell. Leviathan open your mouth, Hell's Mouth, open the gates of Hell here and now: Leviathan opens it's mouth the gates of Hell are open wide open. I summon through the gates Baal first King of Hell, commander of 66 legions of demons, Paimon, King of Hell, commander of 200 legions of demons, Beleth King of Hell, commander of 85 legions of demons, Purson King of Hell, commander of 22 legions of demons, Asmodai King of Hell, commander of 72 legions of spirits, Vine King of Hell, commander of 36 legions of demons, Balam King of Hell, commander of 40 legions of demons, Zagan Great King and President of Hell, commander of 33 legions of demons and Belial King of Hell, he with 80 legions of demons and 50 legions of spirits at his

26

command. I ask that the first King of Hell Baal, King Paimon, King Beleth, King Purson, King Asmodai, King Vine, King Balam, Great King Zagan, and King Belial step through the gateway to this world: First King Baal, King Paimon, King Beleth, King Purson, King Asmodai, King Vine, King Balam, Great King Zagan, and King Belial do step through to this world. All Kings of Hell I ask that you use all of your power to make me impossible to harm and this is what I ask of you all. First King Baal, King Paimon, King Beleth, King Purson, King Asmodai, King Vine, King Balam, Great King Zagan, and King Belial agree to help and departs back through the gates. Leviathan powerful devil, great monster, you whose mouth is the very gateway to Hell itself. Leviathan I ask that you shut your mouth the Hell Mouth that which is the gates of Hell. Leviathan close your mouth, Hell's Mouth, shut the gates of Hell here and now: Leviathan closes it's mouth the gates of Hell are closed. So it is and will be.

You are now more powerful, stronger and harder to harm and these are all beneficial. In many ways we tend to wait until something goes wrong to strengthen ourselves. But it is also true that we need to get benefits from our actions and so do realize that being fit and happy are good aims at any time. I will also add that we will find that strength and power opens up opportunities we normally would not have and opportunities are choice and having choices is to be free while a man or woman: or transgender: with no choices is quite often in reality a slave: yes these do exist in their traditional form, old slavery is just as much a reality as new forms of slavery.

Chapter 4 Power and strength for other people

The magick in this chapter is for you to be able to help other people. I know that for some people right now this may not be worthwhile at all because there is no one that needs this help or that they feel they care about enough. However eventually it is likely that there will be someone they care for and so the first magick of this chapter is to empower a chosen person.

All Kings of Hell magick to empower a chosen person

Leviathan powerful devil, great monster, you whose mouth is the very gateway to Hell itself. Leviathan I ask that you open your mouth the Hell Mouth that which is the gates of Hell. Leviathan open your mouth, Hell's Mouth, open the gates of Hell here and now: Leviathan opens it's mouth the gates of Hell are open wide open. I summon through the gates Baal first King of Hell, commander of 66 legions of demons, Paimon, King of Hell,

commander of 200 legions of demons, Beleth King of Hell,

commander of 85 legions of demons, Purson King of Hell,

commander of 22 legions of demons, Asmodai King of Hell,

commander of 72 legions of spirits, Vine King of Hell, commander

of 36 legions of demons, Balam King of Hell, commander of 40

legions of demons, Zagan Great King and President of Hell,

commander of 33 legions of demons and Belial King of Hell, he

with 80 legions of demons and 50 legions of spirits at his

command. I ask that the first King of Hell Baal, King Paimon, King

Beleth, King Purson, King Asmodai, King Vine, King Balam,

Great King Zagan, and King Belial step through the gateway to this

world: First King Baal, King Paimon, King Beleth, King Purson,

King Asmodai, King Vine, King Balam, Great King Zagan, and

King Belial do step through to this world. All Kings of Hell I ask

that you use all of your power to empower state name of chosen

person make them greatly powerful and this is what I ask of you all. First King Baal, King Paimon, King Beleth, King Purson, King Asmodai, King Vine, King Balam, Great King Zagan, and King Belial agree to help and departs back through the gates. Leviathan powerful devil, great monster, you whose mouth is the very gateway to Hell itself. Leviathan I ask that you shut your mouth the Hell Mouth that which is the gates of Hell. Leviathan close your mouth, Hell's Mouth, shut the gates of Hell here and now: Leviathan closes it's mouth the gates of Hell are closed. So it is and will be.

There are times when we need others to be strong and so I offer magick to help and here it is. But the words here must be spoken aloud while desiring them to help so that they will. But if you do this you will indeed strengthen them and so do use this magick and be helpful to another person.

All Kings of Hell magick to strengthen a chosen person

Leviathan powerful devil, great monster, you whose mouth is the very gateway to Hell itself. Leviathan I ask that you open your mouth the Hell Mouth that which is the gates of Hell. Leviathan open your mouth, Hell's Mouth, open the gates of Hell here and now: Leviathan opens it's mouth the gates of Hell are open wide open. I summon through the gates Baal first King of Hell, commander of 66 legions of demons, Paimon, King of Hell, commander of 200 legions of demons, Beleth King of Hell, commander of 85 legions of demons, Purson King of Hell, commander of 22 legions of demons, Asmodai King of Hell, commander of 72 legions of spirits, Vine King of Hell, commander of 36 legions of demons, Balam King of Hell, commander of 40 legions of demons, Zagan Great King and President of Hell, commander of 33 legions of demons and Belial King of Hell, he with 80 legions of demons and 50 legions of spirits at his

32

command. I ask that the first King of Hell Baal, King Paimon, King Beleth, King Purson, King Asmodai, King Vine, King Balam, Great King Zagan, and King Belial step through the gateway to this world: First King Baal, King Paimon, King Beleth, King Purson, King Asmodai, King Vine, King Balam, Great King Zagan, and King Belial do step through to this world. All Kings of Hell I ask that you use all of your power to make <u>state name of chosen person</u> stronger and this is what I ask of you all. First King Baal, King Paimon, King Beleth, King Purson, King Asmodai, King Vine, King Balam, Great King Zagan, and King Belial agree to help and departs back through the gates. Leviathan powerful devil, great monster, you whose mouth is the very gateway to Hell itself. Leviathan I ask that you shut your mouth the Hell Mouth that which is the gates of Hell. Leviathan close your mouth, Hell's Mouth, shut the gates of Hell here and now: Leviathan closes it's mouth the gates of Hell are closed. So it is and will be.

This following magick is to affect people as a group and this is done via their location. This means that you need to choose some location that is familiar to you or else look at it on maps and look at any pictures you can find of it before performing the magick that follows. This magick is good because you could for instance use it to strengthen a load of people simultaneously and make the weak strong and for instance helps them overthrow oppression. You could make the would be losers into the winners; magick less than this has altered the courses of history.

All Kings of Hell magick to strengthen everyone at a chosen location

Leviathan powerful devil, great monster, you whose mouth is the very gateway to Hell itself. Leviathan I ask that you open your mouth the Hell Mouth that which is the gates of Hell. Leviathan open your mouth, Hell's Mouth, open the gates of Hell here and now: Leviathan opens it's mouth the gates of Hell are open wide open. I summon through the gates Baal first King of Hell,

commander of 66 legions of demons, Paimon, King of Hell,

commander of 200 legions of demons, Beleth King of Hell,

commander of 85 legions of demons, Purson King of Hell,

commander of 22 legions of demons, Asmodai King of Hell,

commander of 72 legions of spirits, Vine King of Hell, commander

of 36 legions of demons, Balam King of Hell, commander of 40

legions of demons, Zagan Great King and President of Hell,

commander of 33 legions of demons and Belial King of Hell, he

with 80 legions of demons and 50 legions of spirits at his

command. I ask that the first King of Hell Baal, King Paimon, King

Beleth, King Purson, King Asmodai, King Vine, King Balam,

Great King Zagan, and King Belial step through the gateway to this

world: First King Baal, King Paimon, King Beleth, King Purson,

King Asmodai, King Vine, King Balam, Great King Zagan, and

King Belial do step through to this world. All Kings of Hell I ask that you use all of your power to strengthen everyone at <u>state</u> <u>chosen address or location</u> and this is what I ask of you all. First King Baal, King Paimon, King Beleth, King Purson, King Asmodai, King Vine, King Balam, Great King Zagan, and King Belial agree to help and departs back through the gates. Leviathan powerful devil, great monster, you whose mouth is the very gateway to Hell itself. Leviathan I ask that you shut your mouth the Hell Mouth that which is the gates of Hell. Leviathan close your mouth, Hell's Mouth, shut the gates of Hell here and now: Leviathan closes it's mouth the gates of Hell are closed. So it is and will be.

Through this magick I have stretched you and through this you have gained a further mental and spiritual reach. I understand that in life all we need is to use our human will alongside some magick and we can alter the world and ourselves. In fact, many people stick to what seems like small problems and gains from this a strong sense of power. But this is not a mistake because often smaller

subtle things have more effect if we consider the vulnerable points

of the obstacles we wish to overcome. But the large grand magick

exists too and yet we will discover that no difference in technique

is necessary at all. In fact, it is true that here the magick has nothing

that is not required and yet you have summoned nine Kings of Hell

and god knows how may legions of demons and spirits. The power

of this comes from you and from the realization that efficiency and

thought are not enemies of occultism they help magick whenever

they are properly introduced.

Chapter 5 Wealth and abundance

In this world we need money and it is difficult to get by without money in some form. It is strange when we consider that my money is paper and base metals that has no inherent value at all and so is worth less than a tap washer materially speaking. But it has a value because society generally has agreed upon the fact that it is worth something and so it is used as a medium of exchange. Have more money work this magick.

All Kings of Hell magick to attract money

Leviathan powerful devil, great monster, you whose mouth is the very gateway to Hell itself. Leviathan I ask that you open your mouth the Hell Mouth that which is the gates of Hell. Leviathan open your mouth, Hell's Mouth, open the gates of Hell here and now: Leviathan opens it's mouth the gates of Hell are open wide open. I summon through the gates Baal first King of Hell, commander of 66 legions of demons, Paimon, King of Hell,

commander of 200 legions of demons, Beleth King of Hell,

commander of 85 legions of demons, Purson King of Hell,

commander of 22 legions of demons, Asmodai King of Hell,

commander of 72 legions of spirits, Vine King of Hell, commander

of 36 legions of demons, Balam King of Hell, commander of 40

legions of demons, Zagan Great King and President of Hell,

commander of 33 legions of demons and Belial King of Hell, he

with 80 legions of demons and 50 legions of spirits at his

command. I ask that the first King of Hell Baal, King Paimon, King

Beleth, King Purson, King Asmodai, King Vine, King Balam,

Great King Zagan, and King Belial step through the gateway to this

world: First King Baal, King Paimon, King Beleth, King Purson,

King Asmodai, King Vine, King Balam, Great King Zagan, and

King Belial do step through to this world. All Kings of Hell I ask

that you attract money to me and this is what I ask of you all. First

King Baal, King Paimon, King Beleth, King Purson, King Asmodai, King Vine, King Balam, Great King Zagan, and King Belial agree to help and departs back through the gates. Leviathan powerful devil, great monster, you whose mouth is the very gateway to Hell itself. Leviathan I ask that you shut your mouth the Hell Mouth that which is the gates of Hell. Leviathan close your mouth, Hell's Mouth, shut the gates of Hell here and now: Leviathan closes it's mouth the gates of Hell are closed. So it is and will be.

Wealth is a different concept to money because wealth isn't a medium of exchange but it represents things that may be investments: things we may make money off owning or selling. I understand that this sounds like a huge too big description and in many ways, it is but through this you will understand that what isn't wealth to one person is to another. Basically, wealth are those things that puts money in your pocket through owning.

All Kings of Hell magick for greater wealth

Leviathan powerful devil, great monster, you whose mouth is the very gateway to Hell itself. Leviathan I ask that you open your mouth the Hell Mouth that which is the gates of Hell. Leviathan open your mouth, Hell's Mouth, open the gates of Hell here and now: Leviathan opens it's mouth the gates of Hell are open wide open. I summon through the gates Baal first King of Hell, commander of 66 legions of demons, Paimon, King of Hell, commander of 200 legions of demons, Beleth King of Hell, commander of 85 legions of demons, Purson King of Hell, commander of 22 legions of demons, Asmodai King of Hell, commander of 72 legions of spirits, Vine King of Hell, commander of 36 legions of demons, Balam King of Hell, commander of 40 legions of demons, Zagan Great King and President of Hell, commander of 33 legions of demons and Belial King of Hell, he with 80 legions of demons and 50 legions of spirits at his

command. I ask that the first King of Hell Baal, King Paimon, King Beleth, King Purson, King Asmodai, King Vine, King Balam, Great King Zagan, and King Belial step through the gateway to this world: First King Baal, King Paimon, King Beleth, King Purson, King Asmodai, King Vine, King Balam, Great King Zagan, and King Belial do step through to this world. All Kings of Hell I ask that you use all of your power to make me richer make greater wealth mine, let wealth in all forms be mine in abundance and this is what I ask of you all. First King Baal, King Paimon, King Beleth, King Purson, King Asmodai, King Vine, King Balam, Great King Zagan, and King Belial agree to help and departs back through the gates. Leviathan powerful devil, great monster, you whose mouth is the very gateway to Hell itself. Leviathan I ask that you shut your mouth the Hell Mouth that which is the gates of Hell. Leviathan close your mouth, Hell's Mouth, shut the gates of Hell

42

here and now: Leviathan closes it's mouth the gates of Hell are closed. So it is and will be.

For many people what they desire could all be summed up with an abundance of all that is good. In fact, this could be thought of as the good life we all talk about and desire. The fact is that magick such as this can help us and this is, I feel the noblest of goals to help ourselves and yes even others. I understand that for some people helping sounds a bit weak and wimpy when it is no such thing. I believe that many of those people whom routinely help others are the real movers and shakers of this world. But there are many ways to help others and ourselves: no lesser thing: and so please help yourself to have abundance of all that is good through this magick.

All Kings of Hell magick for abundance

Leviathan powerful devil, great monster, you whose mouth is the very gateway to Hell itself. Leviathan I ask that you open your mouth the Hell Mouth that which is the gates of Hell. Leviathan

open your mouth, Hell's Mouth, open the gates of Hell here and

now: Leviathan opens it's mouth the gates of Hell are open wide

open. I summon through the gates Baal first King of Hell,

commander of 66 legions of demons, Paimon, King of Hell,

commander of 200 legions of demons, Beleth King of Hell,

commander of 85 legions of demons, Purson King of Hell,

commander of 22 legions of demons, Asmodai King of Hell,

commander of 72 legions of spirits, Vine King of Hell, commander

of 36 legions of demons, Balam King of Hell, commander of 40

legions of demons, Zagan Great King and President of Hell,

commander of 33 legions of demons and Belial King of Hell, he

with 80 legions of demons and 50 legions of spirits at his

command. I ask that the first King of Hell Baal, King Paimon, King

Beleth, King Purson, King Asmodai, King Vine, King Balam,

Great King Zagan, and King Belial step through the gateway to this world: First King Baal, King Paimon, King Beleth, King Purson, King Asmodai, King Vine, King Balam, Great King Zagan, and King Belial do step through to this world. All Kings of Hell I ask that you use all of your power to give me an abundance of all that is good, make abundance mine and this is what I ask of you all. First King Baal, King Paimon, King Beleth, King Purson, King Asmodai, King Vine, King Balam, Great King Zagan, and King Belial agree to help and departs back through the gates. Leviathan powerful devil, great monster, you whose mouth is the very gateway to Hell itself. Leviathan I ask that you shut your mouth the Hell Mouth that which is the gates of Hell. Leviathan close your mouth, Hell's Mouth, shut the gates of Hell here and now: Leviathan closes it's mouth the gates of Hell are closed. So it is and will be.

I feel that as you progress through the book you also gain in how you see the world. I say this because the world has many more things in it than you were led to believe. In fact, knowing that occultism exists as a subject helps you to understand some people better and gives an alternative explanation and set of knowledge to draw on. In fact, I feel that occultists are more adaptable than other people and certainly I do not feel anyone would become less adaptable by learning occultism. In fact, it would help to give more plasticity to their thoughts meaning that they could think of many more things than before.

Chapter 6 Good luck

Good luck is more than slightly helpful because at its most potent it can make riches, help us stay alive and destroy problems. However, I will first concentrate on general good luck the type that will have some effect on anything and everything. But do remember that to do this requires you to will and intend magick to be worked. However, if you do this you will find magick has been worked.

All Kings of Hell magick for good luck

Leviathan powerful devil, great monster, you whose mouth is the very gateway to Hell itself. Leviathan I ask that you open your mouth the Hell Mouth that which is the gates of Hell. Leviathan open your mouth, Hell's Mouth, open the gates of Hell here and now: Leviathan opens it's mouth the gates of Hell are open wide open. I summon through the gates Baal first King of Hell, commander of 66 legions of demons, Paimon, King of Hell,

commander of 200 legions of demons, Beleth King of Hell,

commander of 85 legions of demons, Purson King of Hell,

commander of 22 legions of demons, Asmodai King of Hell,

commander of 72 legions of spirits, Vine King of Hell, commander

of 36 legions of demons, Balam King of Hell, commander of 40

legions of demons, Zagan Great King and President of Hell,

commander of 33 legions of demons and Belial King of Hell, he

with 80 legions of demons and 50 legions of spirits at his

command. I ask that the first King of Hell Baal, King Paimon, King

Beleth, King Purson, King Asmodai, King Vine, King Balam,

Great King Zagan, and King Belial step through the gateway to this

world: First King Baal, King Paimon, King Beleth, King Purson,

King Asmodai, King Vine, King Balam, Great King Zagan, and

King Belial do step through to this world. All Kings of Hell I ask

that you use all of your power to give me good luck make good

luck be mine always and this is what I ask of you all. First King

Baal, King Paimon, King Beleth, King Purson, King Asmodai, King Vine, King Balam, Great King Zagan, and King Belial agree to help and departs back through the gates. Leviathan powerful devil, great monster, you whose mouth is the very gateway to Hell itself. Leviathan I ask that you shut your mouth the Hell Mouth that which is the gates of Hell. Leviathan close your mouth, Hell's Mouth, shut the gates of Hell here and now: Leviathan closes it's mouth the gates of Hell are closed. So it is and will be.

People get rich gambling: although far more get poorer playing them. But it is always good to have some good luck on our side and so I here offer magick to help you. The truth is magick is supposed to help us and we it. I feel that the way the media and other institutions have tried to keep people away from occultism has been damaging. I also understand that sometimes it has occurred that physicists brag of what they have achieved and ask that great proof occultism has achieved anything. I therefore say what would have achieved if you had not the trillions of dollars of funding they have. No real magick will need in some time to get more funding and then we will see what results. We shall make up multi-disciplinary teams and use these as the way we progress: and progress we shall.

All Kings of Hell magick for good luck at games of chance

Leviathan powerful devil, great monster, you whose mouth is the very gateway to Hell itself. Leviathan I ask that you open your mouth the Hell Mouth that which is the gates of Hell. Leviathan open your mouth, Hell's Mouth, open the gates of Hell here and now: Leviathan opens it's mouth the gates of Hell are open wide open. I summon through the gates Baal first King of Hell, commander of 66 legions of demons, Paimon, King of Hell, commander of 200 legions of demons, Beleth King of Hell, commander of 85 legions of demons, Purson King of Hell, commander of 22 legions of demons, Asmodai King of Hell, commander of 72 legions of spirits, Vine King of Hell, commander of 36 legions of demons, Balam King of Hell, commander of 40 legions of demons, Zagan Great King and President of Hell, commander of 33 legions of demons and Belial King of Hell, he with 80 legions of demons and 50 legions of spirits at his command. I ask that the first King of Hell Baal, King Paimon, King Beleth, King Purson, King Asmodai, King Vine, King Balam, Great King Zagan, and King Belial step through the gateway to this world: First King Baal, King Paimon, King Beleth, King Purson, King Asmodai, King Vine, King Balam, Great King Zagan, and King Belial do step through to this world. All Kings of Hell I ask that you use all of your power to give me gambling good luck so I will be lucky at games of chance and this is what I ask of you all. First King Baal, King Paimon, King Beleth, King Purson, King Asmodai, King Vine, King Balam, Great King Zagan, and King Belial agree to help and departs back through the gates. Leviathan powerful devil, great monster, you whose mouth is the very gateway to Hell itself. Leviathan I ask that you shut your mouth the Hell Mouth that which is the gates of Hell. Leviathan close your mouth, Hell's Mouth, shut the gates of Hell here and now: Leviathan closes it's mouth the gates of Hell are closed. So it is and will be.

I want you to enjoy your magick and yet it is true that magick such as this often makes people frightened at first. However, don't be because you are in control of everything and if this magick was harmful the amount of it I have written is huge and so I would be dead by now: I am still alive hooray. However, don't think that magick must be approached with a grey man approach, no you can try new things: if you can accept the dangers of doing so. In reality often trying something new just shows us something about ourselves and what we should do and expands our capabilities. I say this because I want you to be all you are capable of. I want all of humanity to become a race of super-people because I feel any advanced civilization would probably be upgrading their population by making sure we all had vitamin pills. I feel that the correct vitamins do help us just as much as many sports supplements. I say this knowing that this time last year I had almost lost the ability to walk through over work and I used occultism and vitamins to get back to full strength: and I feel I am fitter now than ever. At the very least take a multivitamin daily.

Chapter 7 Success

I will now show you some magick that will help you gain success in all ways. That's right this is magick for general success and so it may help you in ways you did not think of. However, being successful surely beats failing all to Hell and so do use this magick: however, the choice is still yours. Here is this wonderful magick.

All Kings of Hell magick for success

Leviathan powerful devil, great monster, you whose mouth is the very gateway to Hell itself. Leviathan I ask that you open your mouth the Hell Mouth that which is the gates of Hell. Leviathan open your mouth, Hell's Mouth, open the gates of Hell here and now: Leviathan opens it's mouth the gates of Hell are open wide open. I summon through the gates Baal first King of Hell, commander of 66 legions of demons, Paimon, King of Hell, commander of 200 legions of demons, Beleth King of Hell, commander of 85 legions of demons, Purson King of Hell,

commander of 22 legions of demons, Asmodai King of Hell,

commander of 72 legions of spirits, Vine King of Hell, commander

of 36 legions of demons, Balam King of Hell, commander of 40

legions of demons, Zagan Great King and President of Hell,

commander of 33 legions of demons and Belial King of Hell, he

with 80 legions of demons and 50 legions of spirits at his

command. I ask that the first King of Hell Baal, King Paimon, King

Beleth, King Purson, King Asmodai, King Vine, King Balam,

Great King Zagan, and King Belial step through the gateway to this

world: First King Baal, King Paimon, King Beleth, King Purson,

King Asmodai, King Vine, King Balam, Great King Zagan, and

King Belial do step through to this world. All Kings of Hell I ask

that you help me become more successful, let great success be mine

and this is what I ask of you all. First King Baal, King Paimon,

King Beleth, King Purson, King Asmodai, King Vine, King Balam,

Great King Zagan, and King Belial agree to help and departs back through the gates. Leviathan powerful devil, great monster, you whose mouth is the very gateway to Hell itself. Leviathan I ask that you shut your mouth the Hell Mouth that which is the gates of Hell. Leviathan close your mouth, Hell's Mouth, shut the gates of Hell here and now: Leviathan closes it's mouth the gates of Hell are closed. So it is and will be.

For some people their career is the most important thing in their lives: they spend more time working or thinking about working than others do too. I know that for some people this magick will not be something they need or even want. However, I also recognize that for those people that would like or even wouldn't mind career success this magick will be both helpful and freeing.

All Kings of Hell magick for career success

Leviathan powerful devil, great monster, you whose mouth is the very gateway to Hell itself. Leviathan I ask that you open your mouth the Hell Mouth that which is the gates of Hell. Leviathan open your mouth, Hell's Mouth, open the gates of Hell here and now: Leviathan opens it's mouth the gates of Hell are open wide open. I summon through the gates Baal first King of Hell, commander of 66 legions of demons, Paimon, King of Hell, commander of 200 legions of demons, Beleth King of Hell, commander of 85 legions of demons, Purson King of Hell, commander of 22 legions of demons, Asmodai King of Hell, commander of 72 legions of spirits, Vine King of Hell, commander of 36 legions of demons, Balam King of Hell, commander of 40 legions of demons, Zagan Great King and President of Hell, commander of 33 legions of demons and Belial King of Hell, he with 80 legions of demons and 50 legions of spirits at his

command. I ask that the first King of Hell Baal, King Paimon, King Beleth, King Purson, King Asmodai, King Vine, King Balam, Great King Zagan, and King Belial step through the gateway to this world: First King Baal, King Paimon, King Beleth, King Purson, King Asmodai, King Vine, King Balam, Great King Zagan, and King Belial do step through to this world. All Kings of Hell I ask that you help career success be mine and this is what I ask of you all. First King Baal, King Paimon, King Beleth, King Purson, King Asmodai, King Vine, King Balam, Great King Zagan, and King Belial agree to help and departs back through the gates. Leviathan powerful devil, great monster, you whose mouth is the very gateway to Hell itself. Leviathan I ask that you shut your mouth the Hell Mouth that which is the gates of Hell. Leviathan close your mouth, Hell's Mouth, shut the gates of Hell here and now: Leviathan closes it's mouth the gates of Hell are closed. So it is and will be.

This magick you will now learn is for you to help someone else: anyone of your choosing. However, it is an advantage if the person is someone you know: perhaps well enough to know their name or some name you call them and know what they look like. But just as with the other magick a strong will must be used so that it can work.

All Kings of Hell magick for a chosen person to be successful

Leviathan powerful devil, great monster, you whose mouth is the very gateway to Hell itself. Leviathan I ask that you open your mouth the Hell Mouth that which is the gates of Hell. Leviathan open your mouth, Hell's Mouth, open the gates of Hell here and now: Leviathan opens it's mouth the gates of Hell are open wide open. I summon through the gates Baal first King of Hell, commander of 66 legions of demons, Paimon, King of Hell, commander of 200 legions of demons, Beleth King of Hell, commander of 85 legions of demons, Purson King of Hell, commander of 22 legions of demons, Asmodai King of Hell, commander of 72 legions of spirits, Vine King of Hell, commander of 36 legions of demons, Balam King of Hell, commander of 40 legions of demons, Zagan Great King and President of Hell, commander of 33 legions of demons and Belial King of Hell, he with 80 legions of demons and 50 legions of spirits at his command. I ask that the first King of Hell Baal, King Paimon, King Beleth, King Purson, King Asmodai, King Vine, King Balam, Great King Zagan, and King Belial step through the gateway to this world: First King Baal, King Paimon, King Beleth, King Purson, King Asmodai, King Vine, King Balam, Great King Zagan, and King Belial do step through to this world. All Kings of Hell I ask that you make state name of chosen person more successful, make great success theirs and this is what I ask of you all. First King Baal, King Paimon, King Beleth, King Purson, King Asmodai, King Vine, King Balam, Great King Zagan, and King Belial agree

60

to help and departs back through the gates. Leviathan powerful devil, great monster, you whose mouth is the very gateway to Hell itself. Leviathan I ask that you shut your mouth the Hell Mouth that which is the gates of Hell. Leviathan close your mouth, Hell's Mouth, shut the gates of Hell here and now: Leviathan closes it's mouth the gates of Hell are closed. So it is and will be.

This magick allows you to choose what you want to be a success at. This magick however is something to be worked up to if you can and you need to think about exactly how you will phrase what you want to be successful at, so that it cannot be misunderstood. But these are things you can do and so here is this magick.

All Kings of Hell magick for success at a chosen thing

Leviathan powerful devil, great monster, you whose mouth is the very gateway to Hell itself. Leviathan I ask that you open your mouth the Hell Mouth that which is the gates of Hell. Leviathan

open your mouth, Hell's Mouth, open the gates of Hell here and now: Leviathan opens it's mouth the gates of Hell are open wide open. I summon through the gates Baal first King of Hell, commander of 66 legions of demons, Paimon, King of Hell, commander of 200 legions of demons, Beleth King of Hell, commander of 85 legions of demons, Purson King of Hell, commander of 22 legions of demons, Asmodai King of Hell, commander of 72 legions of spirits, Vine King of Hell, commander of 36 legions of demons, Balam King of Hell, commander of 40 legions of demons, Zagan Great King and President of Hell, commander of 33 legions of demons and Belial King of Hell, he with 80 legions of demons and 50 legions of spirits at his command. I ask that the first King of Hell Baal, King Paimon, King Beleth, King Purson, King Asmodai, King Vine, King Balam, Great King Zagan, and King Belial step through the gateway to this world: First King Baal, King Paimon, King Beleth, King Purson,

King Asmodai, King Vine, King Balam, Great King Zagan, and King Belial do step through to this world. All Kings of Hell I ask that you help me become more successful at <u>state what you want to be more successful at</u> let this success be mine and this is what I ask of you all. First King Baal, King Paimon, King Beleth, King Purson, King Asmodai, King Vine, King Balam, Great King Zagan, and King Belial agree to help and departs back through the gates. Leviathan powerful devil, great monster, you whose mouth is the very gateway to Hell itself. Leviathan I ask that you shut your mouth the Hell Mouth that which is the gates of Hell. Leviathan close your mouth, Hell's Mouth, shut the gates of Hell here and now: Leviathan closes it's mouth the gates of Hell are closed. So it is and will be.

You are quite near to the end of this book because there is only one chapter to go and yet finishing this book is what sets us aside from the others who will not follow the path all the way. However, you need not be that person and this in my opinion is good because in life there is often great advantages in finishing that which we wish to gain because it is through this that we often succeed. However, there are things that are made to quit such as those negative things and that which would defeat us because not any one of us should be defeated if it can be avoided. This is why for many people success and victory are close things.

Chapter 8 Friendship and love

I know that friendship is important and we are very blessed that in this age we can have friends in our physical life and online through social media and emails and even live video streaming. I think that these all count as being important human interactions and with this in mind I offer magick for more friends knowing that these could be of any sort that you personally class as friends: magick follows.

All Kings of Hell magick for more friends

Leviathan powerful devil, great monster, you whose mouth is the very gateway to Hell itself. Leviathan I ask that you open your mouth the Hell Mouth that which is the gates of Hell. Leviathan open your mouth, Hell's Mouth, open the gates of Hell here and now: Leviathan opens it's mouth the gates of Hell are open wide open. I summon through the gates Baal first King of Hell, commander of 66 legions of demons, Paimon, King of Hell,

commander of 200 legions of demons, Beleth King of Hell,

commander of 85 legions of demons, Purson King of Hell,

commander of 22 legions of demons, Asmodai King of Hell,

commander of 72 legions of spirits, Vine King of Hell, commander

of 36 legions of demons, Balam King of Hell, commander of 40

legions of demons, Zagan Great King and President of Hell,

commander of 33 legions of demons and Belial King of Hell, he

with 80 legions of demons and 50 legions of spirits at his

command. I ask that the first King of Hell Baal, King Paimon, King

Beleth, King Purson, King Asmodai, King Vine, King Balam,

Great King Zagan, and King Belial step through the gateway to this

world: First King Baal, King Paimon, King Beleth, King Purson,

King Asmodai, King Vine, King Balam, Great King Zagan, and

King Belial do step through to this world. All Kings of Hell I ask

that you help me have more friends, let many friends be mine and

this is what I ask of you all. First King Baal, King Paimon, King

Beleth, King Purson, King Asmodai, King Vine, King Balam, Great King Zagan, and King Belial agree to help and departs back through the gates. Leviathan powerful devil, great monster, you whose mouth is the very gateway to Hell itself. Leviathan I ask that you shut your mouth the Hell Mouth that which is the gates of Hell. Leviathan close your mouth, Hell's Mouth, shut the gates of Hell here and now: Leviathan closes it's mouth the gates of Hell are closed. So it is and will be.

None of us should be without some form of love: love is an important human trait. I however do not just lament on a lack of love others may experience I help them and everyone else to have more love through this next magick. I understand that magick can attract love to you and so I will now show you how: will what follows to work and it shall.

All Kings of Hell magick to attract love

Leviathan powerful devil, great monster, you whose mouth is the very gateway to Hell itself. Leviathan I ask that you open your mouth the Hell Mouth that which is the gates of Hell. Leviathan open your mouth, Hell's Mouth, open the gates of Hell here and now: Leviathan opens it's mouth the gates of Hell are open wide open. I summon through the gates Baal first King of Hell, commander of 66 legions of demons, Paimon, King of Hell, commander of 200 legions of demons, Beleth King of Hell, commander of 85 legions of demons, Purson King of Hell, commander of 22 legions of demons, Asmodai King of Hell, commander of 72 legions of spirits, Vine King of Hell, commander of 36 legions of demons, Balam King of Hell, commander of 40 legions of demons, Zagan Great King and President of Hell, commander of 33 legions of demons and Belial King of Hell, he with 80 legions of demons and 50 legions of spirits at his

command. I ask that the first King of Hell Baal, King Paimon, King Beleth, King Purson, King Asmodai, King Vine, King Balam, Great King Zagan, and King Belial step through the gateway to this world: First King Baal, King Paimon, King Beleth, King Purson, King Asmodai, King Vine, King Balam, Great King Zagan, and King Belial do step through to this world. All Kings of Hell I ask that you attract love to me in abundance and this is what I ask of you all. First King Baal, King Paimon, King Beleth, King Purson, King Asmodai, King Vine, King Balam, Great King Zagan, and King Belial agree to help and departs back through the gates. Leviathan powerful devil, great monster, you whose mouth is the very gateway to Hell itself. Leviathan I ask that you shut your mouth the Hell Mouth that which is the gates of Hell. Leviathan close your mouth, Hell's Mouth, shut the gates of Hell here and now: Leviathan closes it's mouth the gates of Hell are closed. So it is and will be.

I feel that many people want more lovers and few people certainly would say they wanted less in any point in time. However, this is not magick for everyone with some people being happy with the relationship they have already. Indeed, maybe it is the case that this magick is a single person's magick: although not necessarily. But whether you use this magick or not is for you to decide choice is the basis of freedom and someone that is not free is a slave and I do not wish to make slaves I wish to free them because slavery exists today just as much as it even did. I would also like to point out that slavery is still alive not just in the form of what is named modern slavery but also in its old form just not everywhere. I hope that you shall never be enslaved.

All Kings of Hell magick for many lovers

Leviathan powerful devil, great monster, you whose mouth is the very gateway to Hell itself. Leviathan I ask that you open your mouth the Hell Mouth that which is the gates of Hell. Leviathan

open your mouth, Hell's Mouth, open the gates of Hell here and now: Leviathan opens it's mouth the gates of Hell are open wide open. I summon through the gates Baal first King of Hell, commander of 66 legions of demons, Paimon, King of Hell, commander of 200 legions of demons, Beleth King of Hell, commander of 85 legions of demons, Purson King of Hell, commander of 22 legions of demons, Asmodai King of Hell, commander of 72 legions of spirits, Vine King of Hell, commander of 36 legions of demons, Balam King of Hell, commander of 40 legions of demons, Zagan Great King and President of Hell, commander of 33 legions of demons and Belial King of Hell, he with 80 legions of demons and 50 legions of spirits at his command. I ask that the first King of Hell Baal, King Paimon, King Beleth, King Purson, King Asmodai, King Vine, King Balam, Great King Zagan, and King Belial step through the gateway to this world: First King Baal, King Paimon, King Beleth, King Purson,

King Asmodai, King Vine, King Balam, Great King Zagan, and

King Belial do step through to this world. All Kings of Hell I ask

that you help me have many lovers and this is what I ask of you all.

First King Baal, King Paimon, King Beleth, King Purson, King

Asmodai, King Vine, King Balam, Great King Zagan, and King

Belial agree to help and departs back through the gates. Leviathan

powerful devil, great monster, you whose mouth is the very

gateway to Hell itself. Leviathan I ask that you shut your mouth the

Hell Mouth that which is the gates of Hell. Leviathan close your

mouth, Hell's Mouth, shut the gates of Hell here and now:

Leviathan closes it's mouth the gates of Hell are closed. So it is and

will be.

You have learnt a lot and yet for those still interested in occultism

there is always more that can be learnt: I S Rob am the author of

over 480 books almost all on occultism: which is more occult

books than anyone else has ever written in history. I like the way occultism strengthens people and makes them better while they remain the same person. Occultism helps their individuality to remain while they are perfected through practicing occultism: real magick. Magick is a form of power and this power can help us gain what we desire and yes also gain more of other types of power. You are stronger than you were and a more knowledgeable person than you were. I understand that life is not all about magick although it seems it can always help us, it will help you gain success and fulfill goals using you non-magical talents also. Magick was always meant to be coupled with your non-magical mundane abilities because this is the most potent, strongest way to get what you desire. Walk with pride you are an occultist.

www.ingramcontent.com/pod-product-compliance
Lightning Source LLC
Chambersburg PA
CBHW052208090426
42741CB00010B/2452